Christopher Columbus

A Musical Play

Book and lyrics by
Joan Macalpine

Music by
Peter Durrent

Samuel French — London
New York - Toronto - Hollywood

© 1994 BY JOAN MACALPINE (BOOK AND LYRICS)

Rights of Performance by Amateurs are controlled by Samuel French Ltd, 52 Fitzroy Street, London W1P 6JR, and they, or their authorized agents, issue licences to amateurs on payment of a fee. **It is an infringement of the Copyright to give any performance or public reading of the play before the fee has been paid and the licence issued.**

The Royalty Fee indicated below is subject to contract and subject to variation at the sole discretion of Samuel French Ltd.

Basic fee for each and every
performance by amateurs   Code G
in the British Isles

The publication of this play does not imply that it is necessarily available for performance by amateurs or professionals, either in the British Isles or Overseas. Amateurs and professionals considering a production are strongly advised in their own interests to apply to the appropriate agents for consent before starting rehearsals or booking a theatre or hall.

ISBN 0 573 05102 X

Please see page iv for further copyright information

CHRISTOPHER COLUMBUS

Commissioned by, and first performed at, the Unicorn School, Kew, in 1992, with the following cast:

King Ferdinand	John Whall
Queen Isabella	Victoria Steane
Christopher Columbus	Duncan Binnie
Pedro	Nicola Stone
Alonso	Emma Brown
Juan	Rachel Pagnamenta
Luis	Victoria Saxton
Fernando	Chloe Spence
Felipe	John Whall
Carlos	Joanna Munday
Paolo	Victoria Steane
Guatigara	Hallam Rice-Edwards
Guacanagari	Kate Sutherland
Caonabo	Ellen Taylor
Andarana	Amy Christiansen
Guarionex	Leanna Baker
Tondarea	Louisa May
Danaloa	Ella Smith

Directed by Joan Macalpine
Musical direction by Brenda Meek

COPYRIGHT INFORMATION

(See also page ii)

This play is fully protected under the Copyright Laws of the British Commonwealth of Nations, the United States of America and all countries of the Berne and Universal Copyright Conventions.

All rights including Stage, Motion Picture, Radio, Television, Public Reading, and Translation into Foreign Languages, are strictly reserved.

No part of this publication may lawfully be reproduced in ANY form or by any means—photocopying, typescript, recording (including video-recording), manuscript, electronic, mechanical, or otherwise—or be transmitted or stored in a retrieval system, without prior permission.

Licences for amateur performances are issued subject to the understanding that it shall be made clear in all advertising matter that the audience will witness an amateur performance; that the names of the authors of the plays shall be included on all programmes; and that the integrity of the authors' work will be preserved.

The Royalty Fee is subject to contract and subject to variation at the sole discretion of Samuel French Ltd.

In Theatres or Halls seating Four Hundred or more the fee will be subject to negotiation.

In Territories Overseas the fee quoted above may not apply. A fee will be quoted on application to our local authorized agent, or if there is no such agent, on application to Samuel French Ltd, London.

VIDEO RECORDING OF AMATEUR PRODUCTIONS

Please note that the copyright laws governing video-recording are extremely complex and that it should not be assumed that any play may be video-recorded for whatever purpose without first obtaining the permission of the appropriate agents. The fact that a play is published by Samuel French Ltd does not indicate that video rights are available or that Samuel French Ltd controls such rights.

CHARACTERS

King Ferdinand
Queen Isabella
Christopher Columbus
Pedro
Alonso
Juan
Luis
Fernando   } Spanish citizens and sailors
Felipe
Carlos
Paolo
Guatigara (the chieftain)
Guacanagari
Caonabo   } Arawak men
Guarionex
Andarana
Tondarea   } Arawak women
Danaloa

The action takes place in Spain, at sea and in the West Indies in 1492

Running time: about fifty minutes, without an interval

MUSICAL NUMBERS   page

1. *We are the Wind* (Arawak)   1
2. *Shanty* (Luis and Sailors)   8
3. *Pepper and Cloves* (Sailors)   17
4. *I Don't Talk Your Talk* (Arawak and Sailors)   23
5. *We Go Swimming Through the Ocean*
   (Arawak and Sailors)   27
6. *It is Over and Done* (Guatigara and Arawak)   32
7. *Finale* (All)   33

The music for this play is on hire from Samuel French Ltd

A cassette of the music may be borrowed, free of charge, to enable prospective producers to hear the songs

PRODUCTION NOTE

Christopher Columbus was written with the age-group ten to fifteen in mind, and designed so that it could be produced with simple technical resources. The size of the cast is flexible. A single class presented it originally, but in a larger company one group could play the Spanish citizens and another the sailors, and the numbers of those groups and of the Arawak could be increased. One example of logic in the expansion of the cast would be to divide the various functions of the sailor Luis (shantyman, ship's officer and interpreter) among three actors.

The music was originally provided by a piano. A drummer might be an asset, but care must be taken that the music does not overpower the singers, two of whom (Luis the shantyman, and Guatigara) need to be able to carry a solo.

Costume should be kept simple, with only Ferdinand and Isabella richly dressed and Columbus provided with an expensive-looking cloak and perhaps a chain for his last entrance. The Spaniards should be in shirts and short tunics, gathered at the waist, with tights and shoes. They become sailors by removing the tights and shoes, rolling up their sleeves and tying kerchiefs round their heads. The Arawak did not, in fact, wear clothes, but for this production were dressed in tunics of a light-weight material. Their arms and legs were bare and they wore headbands. The Arawak looked on gold as a pretty ornament, so each of them should have a touch of it somewhere—on a headband or belt, or as a clasp or ring. Most importantly, the actors should not look clean. Dirty feet and legs are especially important.

Staging was originally in the round. The acting area was oblong—if you have a large cast you will need an area which is about 14' x 21' (4.3m X 6.4m), and for a smaller cast a slightly smaller space. There were two entrances; the one used by the Arawak led only to a screened-off space and the other to a changing room. The play's structure allows the actors to mime most of the props, although some props will be necessary. Refer to page 36 for set and prop details.

One advantage of playing in the round is that it works geographically. The Spaniards had their entrance, to the east of the area, and the Arawak theirs, to the west. When Columbus set sail, his ship was heading westwards, and when the ships sailed around the islands, singing *We Go Swimming Through the Ocean*, they followed geographical logic.

Working in the round comes more easily to young actors than playing on an end-stage, and it is surprising how many members of the audience can be fitted into a few rows round a central area (though the back rows should be raised if possible). If circumstances dictate that you must use an end-stage, the change is easily made. Take east as upstage, west as downstage, north as stage right and south as stage left, and the moves in the script will work.

The original production (with a cast of eleven and twelve-year-olds) was rehearsed intensively at the end of term when exams were over. From Thursday of one week to Friday of the next, the company spent the whole of each school day working on it, and the following Monday had a Dress Rehearsal and then their first performance. If that can be managed it makes for an immense growth in concentration and commitment and the whole experience becomes deeper and more rewarding. But it does involve considerable goodwill from the staff who would normally be using the hall!

HISTORICAL BACKGROUND

Until the time of Columbus and the other great voyagers, travel had been land-centred, with voyages largely limited to coastal and river traffic. (St Paul found how risky it was to lose sight of land, even in so small a sea as the Mediterranean.) Europe was also a relatively minor player on the world stage, compared with China and Islamic nations, but the traders and navigators of the coming century were to usher in a new epoch of European enterprise and power.

The classical Greeks had shown that the world was a sphere, and the Renaissance brought a revival of interest in their ideas. There must, all through the Middle Ages, have been rumours of a land beyond the Ocean Sea (the Atlantic)—the Vikings had sailed to America from Iceland, and in the 14th and 15th centuries ships from the Hanseatic states and from England kept up the Iceland trade. It is just possible that Bristol ships had reached America before 1492. Further south, the Canaries, Madeira, and the Azores had been discovered in the 14th century—and the Azores are a good third of the way to America. With improved ships and navigation sailors were becoming more adventurous. But the real spur to exploration came from the conquest by the Arabs of the great trade-routes which brought silk and spices overland from the east to Europe. The great merchant cities of the Mediterranean declined in wealth and importance and the Portuguese set out to discover a new way to the east, round the coast of Africa.

It was the Portuguese who developed the ships which enabled Columbus to launch out on a distant journey, especially the light and speedy caravels which had lateen sails and three masts, and were able to cope with adverse winds. Meanwhile sailors from ports on the south-west coast of Spain, from the Portuguese border to Cape Trafalgar, were busy trading with the Canaries and growing in confidence and skill. One of these ports was Palos, where Columbus was to find his ships and seamen.

Columbus was a nobody, born in Genoa, who had bummed around the Mediterranean, north-west Europe, Madeira and Lisbon, picking up mariners' stories and noticing strange bits of flotsam washed up on Atlantic shores. He was self-taught in all he knew and came first to

Portugal, peddling his dream of the way westwards to the Indies. But the Portuguese were growing wealthy through their trade around Africa and all their ambitions were fixed on the eastern route around the Cape of Good Hope. They saw no profit in committing their ships to a hazardous venture westwards, so Columbus went to Spain, where he visited the southwestern ports and won the backing of the Duke of Medinaceli, who owned one of them. The Duke was a kinsman of Queen Isabella and brought Columbus to court. Spanish bureaucracy moved slowly in considering the enterprise and it was not until 1492, when the Moors had at last been driven out of the newly-united kingdom of Spain, that the Queen was able to throw her prestige behind the project and Columbus could set sail.

He had under his command three ships: the *Niña*, the *Pinta* and the *Santa Maria*. The *Niña* and the *Pinta* were handy little caravels - the *Niña* with a crew of twenty-four men and the *Pinta* with twenty-six. They were owned by brothers from the Pinzon family of Palos, with crews who had long served with their captains. The *Santa Maria* was a larger, clumsier ship with a scratch crew of forty men, a few of whom had come from the local prisons. This probably explains why, on the voyage out, there was some trouble aboard the *Santa Maria*, but not aboard the caravels.

So many years of trying to sell his one great idea had hardened in Columbus a determination to succeed and to reap every possible reward for the long years of poverty and humiliation. He had written into his contract with Ferdinand and Isabella all the rewards mentioned in the script, but there was one other which is only alluded to. A pension was promised to the sailor who first sighted land. Columbus's insistence that he was that sailor robbed an ordinary seaman of a good income for life.

To the end of his days Columbus believed that he had discovered the Indies, so he called the people there Indians. But they were in fact the Arawak, South American in stock and culture. They were numerous and they lived well, without having to work very hard. They were highly skilled in making and handling canoes and were excellent fishermen by sea and in the rivers. They dug turtle eggs out of their sandy beaches. They hunted animals and birds. They cultivated the thin soil by heaping it into mounds and planting several different root crops in each mound—one of them being the sweet potato and another manioc, which could be used to make cassava bread. Once the mounds were planted, there was no special harvest time—the weeds were kept under control and whatever was needed each day was dug out without harming the plants.

Around the clean and well-kept huts in their villages, the Arawak also grew some other plants, one of which was maize. They had tobacco, but

Historical Background

were one of the few peoples in the world who had not developed any alcoholic drink. The Spaniards said that they found them to be gentle, generous and hospitable, and noticed that they were unwarlike and had no weapons.

Within fifty years they had been wiped out. It was not that the Spaniards wanted to harm them, but they blundered along, not trying to understand the Arawak but seeing them as an inferior, subject people, to be taught Spanish ways and made to defer to Spanish rule. The first tragedy came about because the *Santa Maria* was wrecked and the two remaining ships could not accommodate all the sailors for the voyage home. Instead of staying peacefully in the fort Columbus built them, and making friends with the Arawak, the men who had been left behind bullied and maltreated the local people, who eventually killed them all.

More trouble was caused by Columbus's failure to understand that the gold which they wore as jewellery came, not from the islands, but from the mainland far to the south-west. He demanded an annual payment from each adult of enough gold dust to fill a hawk's bell—an impossible amount.

Instead of respecting Arawak farming methods, which had for centuries maintained the balance of nature, the Spaniards tried to cultivate the land in their own way. This was unsuitable for the soil, with seeds brought from home, which did not flourish in the different climate. They introduced pigs and dogs, which ran wild among the islands and wiped out the indigenous animals as well as rooting up the Arawak crops. Worst of all, they tried to make the Arawak live according to the Spanish social order, breaking up their traditional tribal structures and demoralising them, and they infected them with European diseases against which they had no immunity and which completed their destruction.

For the Arawak, the coming of Spain was a catastrophe, but perhaps we ought to look on it as only the fastest and most cataclysmic of many movements of people. At one or two of the most remote and inhospitable parts of the islands, archaeologists have found traces of a more primitive people who must have been gradually pushed out of the good land by the Arawak as, over the centuries, they moved in. And in the years leading up to the Spanish conquest, another people, the warlike Carib tribes, had begun to move out of what is now Venezuela to take over the Lesser Antilles. If the Spaniards had not come, the Arawak might eventually have had to face them as a threat.

Guatigara was the first chieftain Columbus encountered when he landed in the Bahamas, and he stands for all the others who welcomed and helped the Spaniards in 1492—he did not, as he does in the script, act as a tourist guide round the islands. But the dates, times and places Columbus visited are correct, and his comments on them come from his report on the voyage.

The years to come brought immense wealth from the Americas to Spain, and to Columbus first riches and then tragedy. This show concerns itself with the early days—the perils and excitement of a great discovery, and a sense of what may go wrong if the discovery is not handled with care and imagination.

CHRISTOPHER COLUMBUS

During the introduction to the opening number, a group of Arawak men, led by their chieftain Guatigara, run on from the west, miming the carrying of a canoe over their heads. They set it down and mime the picking up of paddles, step into the canoe and hold the paddles over their heads as they shout

Arawak   Yah-hey!

They kneel down and begin to paddle the canoe

Music 1: We are the Wind

> We are the wind in the woods on the waves in the
> waters' fall,
> Hear the wind crying.
> We are the birds in the trees, on the hills as they cry and
> call,
> Here we are flying.

They slow down, some of them looking back to watch for the breaker which will lift their canoe onto the beach

> And slow, and slow, and steady as we go
> By the shallows to the shore, to the land.
> And here she comes, the wave that will grow
> To a breaker that will lift us to the land.

The breaker comes and with a surge of paddling they ride it to the beach

> Yah-hey!

They beach the canoe, get out, stow the paddles and divide into little groups to work

Cast your net in the water
There is plenty to be found.
Heap the earth for the planting
There is plenty in the ground.

Turtle eggs on the seashore
There are plenty and to spare.
Birds fly bright in the forest
There is plenty in the air.

Yah-hey!

They group at the west end of the stage and move towards the east, ceremonially bringing offerings of food they have caught, grown and found

And here we come, with plenty in our hands,
To the giver of the land, of the trees.
The wind blows home from water-meet-the-sky
And the sun it is born in the sea.

Guatigara, who is leading, takes off a necklace of wooden beads and holds it up as part of his act of praise

Praise for the wind and the woods and the waves and the
                                waters' fall
For the wind crying.
Praise for the birds, for the trees, for the hills, for the
                                mountain tall
Living and dying.

Yah-hey!

The Arawak run off, west. As he goes, Guatigara drops the necklace

Columbus runs on from the east and picks it up. Pedro and Fernando follow him on

Columbus I have found things. There have been strange things washed ashore from the west. (*He turns to face Pedro and Fernando*) I was born in Genoa, city of Italy, city of the Middle Sea, but when I was born,

Christopher Columbus

> Genoa's day was past. Day of the Middle Sea over. Now it's the Ocean Sea to westwards.
>
> **Pedro** Ocean Sea belongs to Portugal.
> **Columbus** South and east it does. But not to westwards.
> **Fernando** What's there west, but water?
> **Columbus** Listen.
> Trader and voyager, I have been north
> To a wet cold island, to the port of Bristol,
> And Bristol merchants, they go west,
> West and north, to iceberg Iceland
> Where the sea freezes, and they still look west
> To Greenland, Markland, the grapes of Vineland.

Alonso enters, east, to listen

> I have been to Guinea, on the coast of Africa,
> Where the wind blows westerly, always westerly,
> To carry us out across the Ocean Sea.
> And out, on the latitude of Spain and Portugal,
> Past Madeira and far to the Azores
> Where the wind blows easterly, to bring us home.

Carlos enters, east, bouncing a ball. Columbus catches it

> The world is a ball, and to reach the Indies
> The Portuguese go south and eastabout
> All round Africa's Cape of Storms.
> But we shall go to the Indies westabout,
> The speedy journey by the Ocean Sea.

Luis, Juan, Ferdinand and Isabella enter, east. Ferdinand and Isabella take their places on the rostrum. Everyone else, scattered about the stage, kneels. Columbus, who is centre west, the opposite side of the area from the King and Queen, holds up the ball towards them

> And there shall be gold and silk and spices,
> Pepper and cloves, cinnamon and nutmeg.
> And the word of God, of Christ Almighty,
> Shall be taught to the souls of your kingdom come.

Carlos goes off, east

Isabella We understand that you have already presented the idea of sailing west to the King of Portugal.
Columbus Yes, ma'am.
Ferdinand And he appointed a Royal Commission to study the proposal.
Columbus Sire.
Isabella And they turned you down.
Columbus Ma'am.
Ferdinand So you come to us.
Columbus Now that you are driving the Moors out of Granada and uniting Spain as King and Queen of a mighty country——
Isabella Which keeps us very busy. It's a long war.
Ferdinand And expensive.
Isabella However...
Columbus Yes, ma'am?
Ferdinand We shall so far favour your intended journey——
Columbus Yes?
Isabella As to appoint a Royal Commission to study your proposal.

Columbus's hopes are dashed. Ferdinand waves a hand towards Alonso, Luis and Juan

Ferdinand A Royal Commission.

Ferdinand and Isabella turn aside and chat to each other. Alonso, Luis and Juan form a Royal Commission, standing in a semi-circle

Carlos runs on, burdened down with a pile of books and papers

Columbus gives the ball to Pedro, who sits on the rostrum with Fernando. Columbus takes the books and papers from Carlos. They are then passed from hand to hand, from Columbus to Alonso, to Luis, to Juan, and then piled back on Carlos, who finds the load increasingly heavy. Nobody opens any of the books or takes time to read any of the papers

Columbus Another Royal Commission. Books.

He hands the books to Alonso

Christopher Columbus

Alonso Books.

He hands them to Luis

Luis Books.

He hands them to Juan

Juan Books.

He dumps them on Carlos. The same thing happens with the other books and papers

Columbus Papers.
Alonso Papers.
Luis Papers.
Juan Papers.
Columbus Ptolemy.
Alonso Ptolemy.
Luis Ptolemy.
Juan Ptolemy.
Pedro Fourteen-eighty-six. Fourteen-eighty-seven. Fourteen-eighty-eight. Royal Commissions take time.
Columbus Aristotle.
Alonso Aristotle.
Luis Aristotle.
Juan Aristotle.
Fernando Fourteen-eighty-eight. Fourteen-eighty-nine. Fourteen-ninety. And as the Court moves around Spain, so does the Royal Commission.

Ferdinand and Isabella make a move. The Commission, struggling to remain in formation, moves in their wake

Columbus Marco Polo.
Alonso Marco Polo.
Luis Marco Polo.
Juan Marco Polo.
Columbus Alfraganus.
Alonso Alfra—— Who?

Columbus Pupil of Plato.
Alonso Pupil of Plato. Alfraganus.
Luis Alfraganus.
Juan Alfraganus.
Columbus Toscanelli. Only ten years dead.
Alonso Toscanelli.
Luis Toscanelli.
Juan Toscanelli.
Alonso Well, now. I think you will be interested in our conclusions.
Columbus Yes?
Alonso I shall be telling their Majesties that we consider this foreigner's promises and offers impossible, vain, and worthy of complete rejection. It is an enterprise so uncertain, so seemingly impossible, that all money invested in it would be lost. We thought you'd like to know.

Alonso, Luis and Juan exit east

Pedro and Fernando get up

Pedro You're done, then.
Fernando Finished.
Pedro Portugal turned you down.
Fernando And now Spain.
Pedro Done.
Fernando Finished.
Columbus No.

He takes the ball back from Pedro

  I shall take my case to the King of France.
Pedro And if he turns you down?
Columbus We'll scrape the barrel. Go to England.
Carlos You want your books back?
Columbus No. (*He puts the ball on top of the books and papers*) You can carry them. Come on. To France.

Pedro and Fernando go off, east

Columbus and Carlos move after them

Isabella Come back.

Columbus turns back and kneels

Carlos goes off

Columbus Your Majesty?
Isabella You have made a lot of unreasonable demands.
Columbus Not unreasonable.
Isabella To be made a nobleman. To hold the office of Admiral of the Ocean Sea, you and your heirs forever. To be Governor General of any lands you discover. To have one tenth of all goods traded.
Columbus A great discovery deserves a great reward.
Isabella And of course you don't get anything if you don't succeed.
Columbus I shall succeed.
Isabella Very well. You shall have our royal patronage.
Columbus Your Majesty.
Isabella That way the banks will sponsor you. To the tune of a big supply ship.
Columbus The *Santa Maria*.
Ferdinand And the town of Palos. You've spent time there.
Columbus It's a good port. Facing west—fine sailors.
Ferdinand They've been caught smuggling. As a punishment, they can provide two caravels.
Columbus The *Niña* and the *Pinta*. Fast little ships, and handy.
Ferdinand Two caravels, with supplies and sailors.
Isabella Get ready, then, and sail. For God and Spain.
Ferdinand And a good return on capital invested.

Ferdinand and Isabella go off, east

Other members of the cast enter as sailors carrying supplies for the voyage. Alonso, Luis, Juan and Carlos enter first, each carrying a barrel. Columbus watches from the sidelines

The stage is now envisaged as a ship, with the rostrum as the bridge. Some of the cast will climb over the bulwarks to receive cargo from the others. They will be miming ropes rigged to the yardarms, hauling barrels and boxes up from the quay, swinging them inboard, lowering them to the deck and taking them to be stowed below

Alonso Fresh water.
Luis Ship's biscuit.
Juan Salted meat.
Carlos Sardines.

Luis, as shantyman, climbs onto the rostrum

Music 2: Shanty

Luis	Oh, I was born in the town of Palos
All	Haul away and lift her home.
Luis	But I was wild, and I was wayward
All	Haul away, for the salt sea foam.

And it's stamp and go as the work gets harder
Heave and go with a heavy load.
Break your back as you stow the cargo
Far to go by the ocean road.

Pedro, Fernando, Felipe, and Paolo enter, burdened

Pedro Beans and rice.
Fernando Wine and oil.
Felipe Flour and cheese.
Paolo Dried fish.

Luis	So I must leave the town of Palos
All	Haul away and lift her home.
Luis	Leave the loves whose hearts I've broken
All	Haul away, for the salt sea foam.

And it's stamp and go as the hours get longer
Break of day till the night is black.
Casks and kegs and the ropes and compass
Far to go and who comes back?

Alonso Planks and spars.
Fernando Swords and guns.
Carlos Pans and candles.
Juan Bells and trinkets.

Luis	And they'll forget, in the town of Palos,
All	Haul away, and sheet her home.
Luis	They loved a wild and wayward rover
	Who sailed away to the great unknown.

As they sing the last verse, those on the quayside climb aboard. Columbus joins Luis on the rostrum and the company links hands in the shape of a ship, with everyone facing west, and Carlos leaning forward as the figurehead. They sway slightly with the movement of the sea

All	And they'll forget, in the town of Palos,
	Haul away, and sheet her home.
	They loved a wild and wayward rover
	Who sailed away to the great unknown.

The group disperses. Paolo becomes the helmsman on the rostrum, holding the spokes of the wheel, and Columbus cons the ship. The seamen settle to work, with such jobs as splicing a rope, coiling a rope, sewing a sail, preparing food and scrubbing the deck—work which is quiet and will not distract from the dialogue

Juan Hey, this is the life! Gentle wind—fresh air—the sun shining. All my luck come together.
Fernando You a landsman?
Juan Yes.
Fernando What you doing here, then?
Juan I was inside.
Fernando Been thieving?
Juan One of my mates was took up for murder, and me and two others tried to spring him.
Fernando Got caught?

Juan nods

Juan So there's four of us landsmen on this ship. If we hadn't volunteered for the crew, we'd have been hanged yesterday. Look at that blue, blue sea.
Columbus Sou'-sou'-west to the Canary Isles, to look for the steady east wind. To refit and bring on board fresh water and fresh provisions.

The introduction to the Shanty *starts. Luis turns to the musical director*

Luis Thank you. We've done that bit.

The music stops

We know it's hard work. (*He steps down from the rostrum*)
Pedro All work's hard, at sea.
Columbus Thursday, September the seventh, fourteen-ninety-two.

As he begins his next sentence, the members of the crew cross themselves and settle to listen to him

In the name of God and of Spain we set sail from the Canaries, heading west for Japan, China and the Indies, carrying with us a letter from their Majesties to the Great Khan, and an interpreter who can speak Hebrew, Chaldean and Arabic. We shall sail steadily on, night and day, for seven hundred leagues, and after that we shall sail by day and heave to by night.
Felipe So that's how far it is.
Juan How far?
Felipe To Japan. He'll heave to at night when he thinks we're nearly there. Don't want to run ashore in the dark.
Columbus By my reckoning, three or four weeks.

Pedro shades his eyes and looks eastwards

Pedro And there goes the land, below the horizon. Which of us will see that land again?
Alonso See the land or not see it, work's always the same, watch and watch about.
Luis Light winds. Set the topsail. Loose out the spritsail.

Some of the men move to haul on ropes and carry out his command

All Set the topsail. Loose out the spritsail.
Columbus Course due west, and steady as she goes.
Paolo Due west, and steady as she goes.
Alonso And watch by watch, we work the ship.
Felipe Pump the bilges, she's a leaky vessel.

Felipe and Pedro position themselves centrally, one at each end of the

Christopher Columbus

horizontal bar of the pump. They begin work, one pushing down as the other comes up

Fernando Wood for the stove, for a smell of cooking. (*He goes to collect wood, takes it to feed his stove and begins to cook dinner*)

Juan Haul in water and scrub the decks. (*He heaves a bucket over the side, hauls in water and sets to work*)

Alonso Make do and mend, where the taffrail's loose. (*Picking up his tools, he moves to the stern of the vessel, and begins the necessary carpentry*)

Luis Where a sail is torn, where a rope needs splicing. (*He sets to work, sewing or splicing*)

Carlos Sluice the decks, or they'll split in the heat. (*He gets another bucket of water and sluices the planks*)

Pedro Pump the bilges, always pumping.

Carlos Grain to feed the Admiral's chickens. (*He takes some grain to the chicken coop*)

Columbus Monday, September the seventeenth. Twelve days at sea. I keep two logs: the true one for my eyes only, and another for the minds of my unsteady crew. If the Indies are farther than I think and they expect, there may be trouble, so I temper the truth for their fears and tell them we have gone fewer miles than we have. By my reckoning we have sailed, today, one-hundred-and-sixty miles. I tell them one-hundred-and-forty-four.

Luis Out on the Ocean Sea, and the long swell lifts us, drops us, rolls us on the water.

The crew's movements echo his words

Juan I don't feel good.
Luis Wind's rising. Take in the spritsail.
All Take in the spritsail.

Three of the men hurry forward (west) to obey

Juan I feel bad.
Felipe Sea's getting up. Pump the bilges.
Juan If I hadn't volunteered. I'd have been hanged last month, and all my troubles over.
Fernando Grub's up. Dinner for the watch below.

He offers Juan his dinner

Tap your biscuit so the weevils come out.
Juan And crawl away.
Fernando Here, landsman. Bean stew with salt pork; and for you: a lovely, juicy lump of fat.

Juan exits hurriedly east

Columbus Thursday, September the twentieth. Fifteen days at sea. And look! Birds, always birds. Pelicans, doves, a wagtail. These are birds of the land. We are not far from land.

Alonso and Luis take over the pumping as other members of the crew gather to eat

Pedro And how do we know where we are? All my life I've been at sea, and it's always been the same: headland to headland, take your bearings on the church steeple, watch the sea change where a river runs out. While you can see the land, you know where you are, but who can tell where we are now?

Columbus has not been listening to Pedro, but his words are an answer to his question

Columbus The height of the stars as they circle overhead. The length of the day on this date of the year. They tell me our latitude, how far north or south we are.
Pedro West, he says, and steady as she goes, near to three weeks now, out of sight of land. So how far west have we gone? How do we tell?
Columbus By the strength of the wind and the run of the current, I tell our speed. I watch the bow wave as it creams along the side of the ship, and judge our speed. By a cord with a weight on the end and knots tied foot by foot its length along. Boy!

Carlos gets up

Carlos Sir?
Columbus Cast the log.

Christopher Columbus

Carlos Aye, aye, sir. (*Carlos picks up the log on its reel and stands forward, facing east, waiting*)
Columbus Now.

Carlos throws the weight overboard and holds the reel, watching as the speed of the ship sweeps the weight eastward. Columbus counts silently

And stop.

Carlos grabs the cord so that no more reels out

Count the knots which have reeled off in that time.

Carlos hauls in the cord and counts

Carlos Six knots, sir.
Columbus Then that is our speed.

Carlos rewinds the cord, puts the log away and returns to his meal

And by knowing how long we have sailed at that speed, by the wind and the stars and watching the great waters, we can tell how far we have travelled each day.
Pedro And we know. Any old sailor knows. How far north or south, we can tell that as we sail by the stars. But how far east or west is by guess and by God, and who can tell, by God, if he's guessing right?
Columbus Monday, September the twenty-fourth. Nineteen days at sea, and a fair wind blowing.

Felipe and Pedro finish their meal. They move west, to the bows of the ship

Felipe This wind never changes.
Pedro Right. So you tell me: how do we get back?
Felipe Tack into the wind.
Pedro And how long that take us? Tacking, all the way home? Food run out, water run out, lash the tiller and come to some port, somewhere, a crew of all dead men.
Felipe And birds from the land. None of them now. Nothing now but wind and clouds and an empty sky.

Columbus They grow fearful, they grow malcontent. Things go better on the *Niña* and the *Pinta*, but on the *Santa Maria* the men huddle and grumble and no man meets my eyes.
Paolo Hey, hey, what's that? Look at that!
Alonso Fish. Fish that fly! Fish, flying aboard!
Paolo Catch them!

The crew jump and reach and dive, trying to catch the slippery fish and hold them

Juan enters and joins them

Alonso joins in the chase

Luis Hey there! Keep pumping.
Paolo Catch them! Fresh fish for supper, mates!
Carlos Got one! Here, I got one!
Alonso I got one——(*It flaps out of his hands*) Here, come back, come back here!
Felipe Here we are! Fresh fish for supper!
Fernando I've a drop of oil not rancid yet. Fried fish all round.
Pedro Fried fish!
Juan Fresh fish!

Alonso returns to the pumping

Alonso Don't forget the workers.
Columbus And they forget their fears for another day.

A shout is heard off stage west

Caller (*off*) Land ho! Land ho!
Columbus Whither away?
Caller (*off*) West-sou'-west and a point west.
Columbus Alter course and steer for it. West-sou'-west and a point west.
Paolo West-sou'-west and a point west.

The crew crowd to look south-west

Juan Can you see?

Christopher Columbus

Alonso No.
Felipe We're too low. Have to be at the masthead.

Carlos jumps up on someone's back

Luis There!
Carlos I can see it! It's land! Land, land, land!
Columbus Tuesday, September the twenty-fifth. The lookout on the *Pinta* sights land.
Carlos Will that be Japan?
Columbus Wednesday, September the twenty-sixth. Sunrise shows us that the land was no more than a bank of clouds.

The men turn away, despondently

Luis Back to work, and pump the bilges.

Fernando and Carlos take over at the pump as everyone returns to work

Columbus Due west, and steady as she goes.
Paolo Due west, and steady as she goes.
Pedro Wednesday, October the third. A month at sea and no land in sight. Three to four weeks, he said.
Columbus Look! Birds! Great flocks of birds. Flying from land, they can only be flying from land.
Pedro And flying to land. Look. They fly south-west. South-west, that's where the land is. South-west.
Felipe That's where the land must be. South-west.

As each crew member speaks, he turns to face Columbus. A sense of menace towards him grows

Fernando South-west.
Juan South-west.
Alonso South-west.
Carlos }
Pedro } (*together*) South-west.

The pumping stops. For a moment, Columbus confronts the men. Then he turns to Paolo

Columbus Steer sou'-west by west and a point west.
Paolo Sou'-west by west and a point west. (*He alters course*)

The crew return to work, grumbling

Pedro October the seventh. Thirty-two days at sea. No land in sight.
Felipe Thirty-three days. No land in sight.
Juan Thirty-four days. No land in sight.
Columbus All hands on deck and stand to hear your Admiral.

The men stand and turn to listen. The pumping stops

> We set out on this voyage for God and for Spain. Before we sailed, you went to church, every man of you. Confessed your sins and took God's blessing for your journey and your safe return. And it has been long—though now we see clear signs in these birds that land is not far off, and we are near to the Indies, to the pepper, the spice, the gold that will make each one of you a man of memory to your children, your great-grandchildren, and to all the town of Palos. But it has been long, and you lose heart, and I think: what have I here on board? Is it men, or mutinous children? Oh yes, you turn on me, for you are many. Tip me into the water one night, and say that I slipped as I took the angle of the stars. Come now. Any three of you could do that, if you took me from behind. But then. Ask yourselves. Well rid of me, you turn for home, but who will get you home? Which of you knows the winds as I know the winds? Reads the ocean as I read the ocean? Which of you can navigate as I can? Who knows where to find the west wind to take you home? No. Not one man here. Your lives are in my hand, and what I say you do. And I say we look up to those birds, we look up to heaven and remember the blessing on us when we set sail, and we sail on. There can be no turning back till we have found Japan and China, the pepper and the gold.

Pause

> And now about your business, and work this ship.

Luis Shake out the topsail. Pump the bilges.

Pause

Juan and Fernando take up the pumping. Felipe and Pedro go to shake out

Christopher Columbus

the topsail. The others take up other jobs about the deck. Carlos takes a bucket on a rope and goes to sling it overboard to fill with water

Pedro Wednesday, October the tenth. Thirty-five days at sea. No land in sight.
Felipe Thursday, October the eleventh——
Carlos Sir! Sir! My Lord Admiral!
Columbus Yes?
Carlos In the water, sir, there's a branch. A branch in the water, sir with leaves on it. Fresh leaves, sir. A branch with fresh leaves floating by.

The men rush to starboard to see the branch as it floats by

Luis Pump the bilges! Pump the bilges, you lubber-headed, pigeon-witted greengrocers! D'you want us to founder, with land about to break the horizon? Shake out a reef in the foresail, and jump lively.

The men return excitedly to work: Juan and Fernando to the pump, Felipe and Pedro to shake out the foresail and then belay the ropes, Alonso to sluice the deck and Carlos to scrub it

Felipe Can't be far off now.
Pedro The Indies.
Alonso The great cities that Marco Polo wrote about.
Carlos The great Khan.
Juan Spices, silk and gold.

Music 3: Pepper and Cloves

All There will be
Pepper and cloves and ginger and nutmeg
Cinnamon, mace and cardamom seeds
Growing like weeds.
And most of all, I know, I've been told
There will be gold.

They build high, high, high to touch the sky
Cities with turrets of gold.
They build low, low, low, where your feet must go
Streets that are paved with gold.

And the market's cheap where they crowd and heap
Spice to be bought and sold.

Going to be the quality, going to be a lord,
Swagger back to home again, coming from abroad,
Cloth of gold upon my back with dandy silken hose,
Rings upon my fingers and a diamond in my nose.

During the final verse, the crew return to their work, telling each other about their prospects

He is great, great, great by the Golden Gate,
Terrible great, that King,
And low, low, low will the Admiral go
Greeting the Khan, the King.
While it's you and me going wild and free
Off on a golden fling.

The crew settle down quietly for the night, with the exception of Paolo at the wheel

Columbus Thursday, October the eleventh. At ten o'clock at night I thought I saw a light in the distance, like a fisherman raising and lowering his lantern, or perhaps someone walking, house to house, along a harbour wall. But none of the crew could see it, so I did not claim it to be a landfall. The moon rose at midnight and at two o'clock in the morning of Friday, October the twelfth, the *Pinta*, which was ahead of us, fired a gun. One of the seamen on board had sighted land in the direction where I had seen the light. I, therefore, was in fact the first of all to sight the land.

The crew can now see the land from the deck

Felipe There it is!
Juan And green! All these days at sea, and now we see green again.
Alonso No city. (*He turns to Columbus*) Can't see a city.
Pedro Not even a village.
Columbus This is an island—all the maps show islands off the coast of Japan. Japan will be over the horizon still, south-west of here, and China beyond that again.

Christopher Columbus

Luis And the natives? Friendly?
Columbus We'll have the ship's boat launched, and as we row in we'll have the cannon trained on shore to cover our landing. Out anchor!
Luis Out anchor! Launch the boat! Man the cannon!

They all go off, east

All   There will be
Pepper and cloves and ginger and nutmeg
Cinnamon, mace and cardamom seeds
Growing like weeds.
And most of all, I know, I've been told
There will be gold.

Tondarea and Andarana run on from the east, carrying a hammock

Tondarea sees something in the distance, to the south-east, and stops, transfixed

Andarana Come on.
Tondarea No, look.

Andarana catches sight of what Tondarea has seen. They drop the hammock

Andarana Are they birds?
Tondarea They've got great, white wings.
Andarana Guarionex!

Guarionex enters

The women point at what they can see

  Are they birds?
Tondarea They're flying low, over the water.
Guarionex No. Not birds.
Tondarea Then what are they?
Guarionex Look: between the wings and the water. They are like great canoes.
Andarana They're too high-built. You couldn't use paddles.

Guarionex You wouldn't need to. Not with those wings.
Tondarea There are creatures on board.
Andarana Like people. But not the same.
Guarionex They've stopped flying. Look. They're folding their wings.
Tondarea And that is a canoe, coming from the biggest one. Making for the beach.
Guarionex Go and tell Guatigara. Quick.

Tondarea runs off

Andarana And look at the way they paddle. They've got their backs to us.

Guacanagari comes on, followed by Caonabo

Guacanagari What are they? Are they people?
Andarana Whatever they are, they come from water-meets-the-sky, where the sun is born, where the rain comes from.
Caonabo Does Guatigara know they're coming?
Andarana We've sent to tell him. Look. They're beaching their canoe.
Guacanagari Should we go to meet them?
Guarionex No. Stay among the trees. Watch, and see what they are doing.

The Arawak retreat, westwards, as if entering a wood, and crouch down

Columbus enters, east, with Luis and Alonso, who has round his waist a string with little bells on it. Fernando, Felipe, Juan and Paolo gather in the entrance, Paolo carrying the banner of Spain

Alonso Look, sir. In among the trees. There are people.
Columbus That's as it should be. We reach the Indies, and here are the Indians. Luis de Torres.
Luis Sir?
Columbus You are here to interpret. Hebrew, Chaldean, Arabic. Let's hear them.
Luis Sir.

He takes a step towards the Arawak. After each greeting, he pauses for a response and receives none

Christopher Columbus

Shalom. Salahan. Allah Akbar. Salve. Salute. Salaam. I'm sorry, sir. Not a flicker.
Columbus They are clearly uneducated. You don't speak Japanese?
Luis No, sir.
Alonso Excuse me, sir. Could I try?
Columbus You speak Japanese?
Alonso It might work without words.
Columbus All right. See what you can do.

Alonso takes a string of bells from his waist and holds them up. He moves them gently, so that they make a delicate tinkling sound. Without looking directly at the Arawak he moves a little closer to them. They are fascinated. Guarionex stands up and slowly moves towards the bells. Alonso detaches one and offers it, holding it out and then putting it down and stepping back. Guarionex creeps up and grabs it, jumping hastily back and stopping when he hears it ring. He and Alonso have a dialogue with the bells, and other Arawak creep out to join them

Guatigara arrives, followed by Tondarea, who is leading Danaloa

The Arawak, when they notice him, defer to Guatigara and watch him come through to face Columbus. Danaloa sits down in a corner

Columbus Aha. Now here we have clearly the chieftain. He might have an education. Try again.
Luis They're savages, sir.
Columbus Try.
Luis Sir. (*With increasing despondency, he searches through all the languages he knows*) Shalom. Salahan. Allah Akbar. Salve. Salute. Salaam. Buon giorno. Bonjour. Um. Hallo?
Columbus Not a lot of use.
Luis I'm sorry, sir. They don't speak any civilised language.
Columbus Going to have to do it with signs.

The audience can understand what each side says to the other, but the characters pick up meaning only from signs and gestures

I offer you my greetings.
Guatigara We, the Arawak, welcome you as our guests.

Columbus You Indians have a beautiful island.
Guatigara This island is called Guanahini. Guanahini.
Columbus I name this island San Salvador. I am Don Christopher Columbus.
Guatigara Christopher Columbus.
Columbus That's right.
Guatigara Guatigara.
Columbus I call on all those present to witness that I take possession of this island of San Salvador for the King and Queen of Spain. (*He beckons Paolo forward with the banner*) In sign of which I take the earth of this island and we lay over it the banner of Spain.

He stoops to take up some earth and Paolo passes the banner over it. Guatigara takes up some earth as Columbus did

Guatigara Yes, it is good land, and because we are his children, God has lent it to us while we live, so long as we take care of it.
Columbus We come to bring you civilisation. At the top of the beach my men are putting up a cross and a gallows, in token that from this time onwards these new-found lands will be ruled by Christian faith and Spanish justice.
Guatigara I see. Wooden posts. That's all right: we have no objection if you need them. But you must be hungry. I hope you will accept our friendship, and come to eat with us. (*He makes a gesture of invitation, indicating that they should go off, west*)
Columbus Is that your village? I will come. (*He turns to Felipe and Juan*) You two: follow on. (*He moves towards the exit, west*)
Luis Are you sure it's safe, sir?

Columbus stops in the exit, and turns to Luis

Columbus These are gentle people. Primitive. I'll be safe. And so will you, if you treat them well and fairly. We've come out of the blue and they think we're some kind of gods. So let them be curious, and make friends with them.

Columbus, Felipe and Juan exit with Guatigara

Pause

Christopher Columbus

Luis Well. Hallo.
Tondarea Do you think they're safe?
Alonso Everyone. Look happy.
Caonabo They're smiling.
Paolo They seem to be friendly.

The Arawak are fascinated by the strange appearance of the newcomers

Guacanagari Their skin is different.
Paolo No sudden movements. Don't want to frighten them.
Fernando That tickles.
Guarionex (*pointing at Alonso's kerchief*) Is there hair under that cloth?
Alonso You want that? Here you are.

He takes the kerchief from his head and hands it over

Guarionex Thank you! Look! (*He shows the kerchief to the other Arawak and then turns back to Alonso*) Thank you.
Caonabo These are good people.
Paolo I like this place. Friendly people.

Music 4: I Don't Talk Your Talk

All I don't talk your talk and you don't talk mine
How will it go?
My friend or my foe?
I look in your face and I look for a sign
How can I know?
What will it show?
Listen to your hands as they spread or entwine
A fist for a blow?
Or peace-giving, so?

Open up your hands to me
Smile a friend as you should be
And the sun comes out
And the wind will shout
What a day
It'll be

Step by step and hand by hand
Who needs words to understand?
For the birds will sing
And the bells will ring
Over sea
Over land

I don't talk your talk and you don't talk mine
How will it go?
My friend or my foe?
I look in your face and I look for a sign
How can I know?
What will it show?
Listen to your hands as they spread or entwine
A fist for a blow?
Or peace-giving, so?

Guarionex gives his headband to Alonso. Tondarea remembers the hammock and gets it

Tondarea Thank you. Here. From us.
Luis What's that?
Tondarea Here. You take it. It's a hamaca. Hamaca.
Luis Hamaca?
Tondarea Look.

A team of Arawak take the ends of the hammock and spread it out

You get in.

Tentatively at first, Luis gets into the hammock

Luis Hey! Look at me! Look at me!
Alonso What's that, then?
Luis It's a hammacka. I'll have this in the ship. This'll be better than sleeping on the deck.

He gets out of the hammock and the Arawak fold it up. Guacanagari notices the knife worn in Paolo's belt

Christopher Columbus

Guacanagari What's that, then? What have you there?
Paolo What, this? It's a knife. You want to see it? Here.

Holding the knife by the blade, he offers it to Guacanagari, who takes it by the handle

Guacanagari You hold it by the wood, but what is this bit?
Paolo Careful! It's sharp.
Guacanagari Look! It's polished. See how it catches the sunlight!
Andarana Let me see.

Andarana takes the knife by its blade

Aah! Ow! It bites. I've been bitten!
Fernando Here. It's not too deep. Let me tie it up. Better put your knife away.

Guatigara and Columbus enter

Luis The crew out there on the ship have got the cannon trained on people who don't even know what a knife is for. (*To Columbus*) It's nothing, sir. Only a cut hand.

Danaloa gets up

Danaloa Guatigara. Guatigara.
Guatigara Yes?
Danaloa There is evil here. No friendship. There is bleeding.
Guatigara There was an accident. It's nothing. The strangers are taking care of the hurt.
Danaloa There is a hard sharpness. There is evil for us in these people.
Guatigara They come from where our life is given. Where the sun is born and the rain drives in. They can only be good.
Danaloa No sun, no rain. These people are a hurricane.
Alonso Look, sir, look.

He shows Columbus the headband Guarionex has given him

See there! That's gold leaf, isn't it?

He indicates some decoration on the headband

Columbus Gold, yes, that's gold. That's what we came for. (*He turns to Guatigara*) Where did this come from?

Guatigara thinks he means the headband, and is puzzled. Columbus sees someone else with gold as a decoration

This. This. Gold. This is gold.
Guatigara Gold.
Columbus Where? Where gold? Gold there? There? There?

He points in different directions

Guatigara Ah. Gold there. (*He points south-west*) A long way off, on the mainland.
Columbus South-west. Of course! The Japanese mainland. And perhaps, between here and the Japanese cities, we shall find the gold mines. Sir. Guati—what's-your-name—I invite you—some of your people—come on board my ship. Come to see our civilisation.
Guatigara To come to your ship? Thank you.

Columbus leads Guatigara off, east

The others follow, chattering excitedly and taking the hammock with them

Danaloa and Tondarea are left alone

Danaloa Oh my people, no. Run and hide. Run and hide.
Tondarea They are strange, but they are good. Listen. It sings. (*She shakes a bell*)
Danaloa It sings one word. It sings death.

Tondarea leads Danaloa off, west

The others enter, east. They are formed up to represent the three ships, each group in a line, one behind the other. Paolo, Guacanagari and Carlos form the **Pinta***, Felipe, Caonabo and Juan the* **Niña** *and Columbus, Guatigara, Andarana and Pedro the* **Santa Maria**

Christopher Columbus

Columbus Up anchor!

Each actor raises his arms so that his hands are a little higher than his face, palms towards him, to represent the sails of a ship

> All sail set, and the Indians will guide us south-west to the gold mines, the cities of gold. Three fine ships.
> **Paolo** The *Pinta*.
> **Felipe** The *Niña*.
> **Columbus** And the *Santa Maria*.

They set off, swaying gently as they go, heading west along the north side of the stage

Music 5: We Go Swimming Through the Ocean

All We go swimming through the ocean, we go sailing
Round the islands—far and free.
And the wind blows, and the sun shines
And the ships dance across the sea.

Columbus speaks over the music between the verses

Columbus A chain of islands, all green, and the vegetation is as in April in Andalusia. And the singing of the birds such that a man might never wish to leave here, and flocks of parrots that obscure the sun.

They have reached the west end of the stage and turn to head south, still moving slowly and waving to occasional islanders ashore

All We go laughing with a greeting and a welcome
Every village—every shore—
And the fish dart to make a rainbow
And the birds wing and swing and soar.
Guatigara Now this is a great island. Cuba.
Columbus Now, this is Japan. The mainland. No city just here, but I never saw anything so beautiful, full of trees surrounding the river, handsome and green and different from ours, with flowers and fruit each in its manner. But the wind changes and the weather grows cooler, so we'll

leave Japan for our next voyage. We'll find the gold as token of our success, and go home.

The ships turn to sail eastwards, the Santa Maria *edging in to end the verse in the centre of the stage*

All We go hunting for the gold and for the riches
Turning east now—coasting slow—
And the greed grows, and the hunger
To be rich men before we go.
Guacanagari The island of Babeque, now. That is a beautiful island. Green trees—great blue lagoon—golden beaches.
Paolo Golden beaches?
Guacanagari Great, long, golden beaches.
Paolo Right. Babeque, here we come.

The Pinta *sets sail for the exit, east*

Columbus Hey! What are you doing?
Paolo See you.

The Pinta *exits east*

Columbus Traitor. Traitor! This is treason.
Guatigara This is Bohio. One of the biggest of the islands.

They lower the sails

Columbus Ah. Yes. I name this the Spanish island. Hispaniola. The best lands in Castile cannot be compared as to beauty or fertility with these. And more and more Indians come to greet us.
Pedro We give them buttons and bits of broken glass or pottery, and they give us ear-rings, nose-rings, nuggets of pure gold.
Columbus But they do not show us where the gold comes from.

They raise the sails again

Felipe Christmas Day, and hard work rounding a promontory. Everyone exhausted. Night comes, with a light breeze.

Christopher Columbus

Columbus Leave the tiller to the helmsman, and all go to sleep.
Pedro And the helmsman wakes a boy, gives him the tiller, and goes to sleep.
Felipe And the current takes the *Santa Maria*.

The "Santa Maria" drifts, and runs aground against the rostrum. The sails come down

"Santa Maria" Help!
Columbus Launch a boat. Haul us off.
Pedro Can't shift her.
Columbus Cut down the mainmast. Jettison the ballast.
Pedro She's stuck fast.

Tondarea, Guarionex and Danaloa enter west

Tondarea What's wrong? What's wrong out there?
Andarana This ship's gone aground. Come and help.
Caonabo Get your canoes. Help them.

Tondarea, Guarionex and Danaloa skirt round the edge of the stage until they reach the rostrum. The Niña *dissolves back into three individuals, and everyone begins to unload the* Santa Maria *onto the rostrum*

Guarionex We're coming.
Tondarea I'll take that barrel.
Guarionex Heave out that sack.
Pedro Barrels.
Juan Sacks.
Felipe Food.
Columbus Guns.
Pedro Ropes.
Juan Spars.
Caonabo Hurry, now. The ship's breaking up.
Columbus Compass and quadrant.
Tondarea Nothing left. We've cleared the ship.
Guarionex Everything safely heaped ashore.

They help the crew of the Santa Maria *onto the rostrum*

Guatigara Well-guarded to keep it safe.
Columbus Thank you. All. Thank you. And now we've got one ship, where we ought to have three.
Juan And if one green bottle should accidentally fall...
Columbus People who make jokes get left behind.
Juan Sorry.

The "Pinta" enters

Paolo Hallo! We're back.

The "Pinta" lowers its sails

Columbus Where've you been?
Paolo Just went to investigate. Only the Indians talked about this island with golden beaches.
Columbus And?
Paolo When they said golden, they meant yellow. Sand, sand, sand.
Columbus There is gold somewhere. These Indians are keeping quiet about where it comes from. But we can get round that. When we come back we'll set up good government, and good government means taxes. Each Indian, once a year, shall bring one of those little bells they like so much, and bring it full of gold dust.
Felipe Maybe there really isn't gold.
Columbus There is gold. What else have we come for? But now: time to go home.
Paolo There won't be room, in two caravels, for all of us.
Columbus No. We'll build a fort, stock it well, and leave the lucky ones to enjoy a holiday in the sun until we get back. Make friends with the Indians. But for the rest of us: home.
Paolo Home!
Felipe Palos!
Pedro Spain!
Carlos My mum!
Columbus I shall be sorry to say good-bye to these gentle, kindly people. But some of them are to come with us. (*He turns to Guatigara, indicating the east*) We go to Spain.
Guatigara To Spain.
Columbus You come to Spain.

Guatigara To Spain? Me? No.
Columbus You come to see our civilisation. To feel the power of Spain. To learn Spanish and to become a Christian, so that you can come back here and convert your people. Next year. You come back.
Guatigara No.
Columbus Get the chieftains and the others will be more docile. We'll take a woman along as well—that blind one, she seems to have some sort of power among them. Come.
Guatigara No. We have helped you. Now you go to Spain. We go to our home.

He turns to go, leading Danaloa

Columbus Get them. Now!

There is a struggle. Guatigara is captured and Pedro begins to tie him up. Danaloa is killed and caught by Felipe as she falls

Paolo goes off, east

The rest of the Arawak retreat towards the west. Holding Danaloa, Felipe confronts Columbus

Felipe Good people. Good people. What call have we to kill them?
Columbus They must learn to obey.

Pause

And it's not as if they were Christians. Throw her overboard. And take him below.

Columbus exits, east, followed by Felipe carrying Danaloa, and by the other Spaniards with the exception of Pedro, who is still tying up Guatigara

A murmuring breaks out among the Arawak

Guarionex Guatigara.
Tondarea Where are you going?

Andarana What must we do?
Guacanagari Will they come for us all?

The murmuring continues, with voices overlapping, and then two voices break out more loudly

Caonabo We'll come to rescue you.
Tondarea We'll get the big canoes and come after you.
Guatigara No. They have swords and guns and knives. And no mercy. You cannot fight them.
Tondarea Then what must we do?

The other Arawak take up the cry

Music 6: It is Over and Done

Guatigara Run. Run and escape.

> It is over and done
> Our day in the sun
> Oh my people run
> And hide.

Arawak
> The sun is setting and the twilight falls
> A frightened creature in the forest calls
> And here in the fear of the coming night
> Who can walk in safety in the failing light?

Guatigara
> For the east wind brings
> Mighty ships with wings
> And the song that it sings
> Is death.

Arawak
> The day is passing and the fire burns low
> How deep the darkness there is none to know
> But here in the fear like awake in dread
> Who can sleep in safety when the fire is dead?

Guatigara
> It is over and done
> Our day in the sun

> Oh my people run
> And hide. (*He repeats the last verse*)

Pedro leads him off, east

The Arawak retreat and go off, west

Fernando and Alonso enter with a crowd of Spaniards to greet Columbus on his return to Spain

Fernando He's coming! He's landed!
Alonso Safely home! But they had to leave some behind.

Luis enters

Luis Columbus is back!
Alonso Safely back, and all's well.

Juan enters

Juan Columbus is back! Ships weighed down with treasure!
Luis He found Japan.
Juan And China and the Indies.

Carlos enters

Carlos Columbus is back! He's coming to meet the King and Queen!
Alonso With gold and silk and spices.
Juan That's what I heard too. We'll all be rich! The whole of Spain rich!

Music 7: Finale

All   There will be
Pepper and cloves and ginger and nutmeg
Cinnamon, mace and cardamom seeds
Growing like weeds.
And most of all, I know, I've been told
There will be gold.

During the next verse, Ferdinand and Isabella enter, to stand on the rostrum, facing west

Columbus enters and moves slowly along the south side of the stage and then to the centre of the west side, to face Ferdinand and Isabella, as far away from them as possible. He carries a ball—the same size as the ball Carlos brought on in the opening scene—on which is painted the world as he believes it to be. He is followed by Guatigara, who stops in the south-west corner, facing the Arawak entrance

> It is Spain, Spain, Spain, will be great again
> Half of the world at its feet,
> And the great, great, great, they are here in state
> Power and glory meet
> When the admiral stands with the world in his hands
> Here in the city street.

The Spaniards freeze as the Arawak sing off stage

Arawak We are the wind in the woods on the waves in the waters' fall
Hear the wind crying.
We are the birds in the trees, on the hills as they cry and
                                                  call
Here we are dying
Dying
Dying.

During the next verse, Columbus lifts the ball high above his head and moves slowly towards Ferdinand and Isabella, the Spaniards on either side of him clapping him as they sing and, as he passes them, turning to kneel facing the King and Queen. By the end of the verse they are all on their knees and he, last of all, kneels down, holding the ball up, offering it to Ferdinand and Isabella. Guatigara does not watch, but stands still, looking off

Spaniards He is great, great, great, as he comes in state
Greeting our Queen, our King
For he knew, knew, knew that his dream was true
Dreamt, and his dreams took wing.
Build the bonfires high, and as he comes by
Bells in the steeples ring.

Christopher Columbus

Formality is dropped as they tell each other the wonderful news about their rosy future

>For there'll be
>Pepper and cloves and ginger and nutmeg
>Cinnamon, mace and cardamom seeds
>Growing like weeds
>And most of all, I know, I've been told
>There will be gold.

The Spaniards repeat the last verse and then freeze as Guatigara sings

Guatigara   Oh my people, run and hide.

THE END

FURNITURE AND PROPERTY LIST

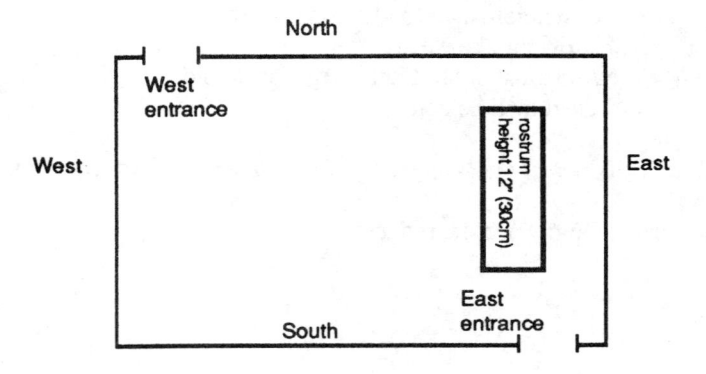

```
                    North
         ┌─────┬────────────────────┬─┐
         │ West│                    │ │
         │ entrance                 │ │
         │          ┌──┐            │ │
   West  │          │rostrum        │ │ East
         │          │height 12" (30cm)│
         │          └──┘            │ │
         │                   East   │ │
         │          South    entrance│
         └──────────────────┴───────┴─┘
```

Further dressing may be added at the director's discretion

Off stage: Ball (a netball is the right size) (**Carlos**)
Books (two or three large, heavy ones, leather-bound) (**Carlos**)
Papers (large, well thumbed bundles) (**Carlos**)
Bells (little hawks' bells, some strung around **Alonso's** waist and others belonging, singly, to other seamen)
Hammock (a simple one, made of cords, not cloth) (**Tondarea**)
Banner of Spain (**Paolo**)
Globe (the same size as the ball, but painted with a map of the world as Columbus believed it to be) (**Columbus**)

Personal: **Guatigara:** necklace of wooden beads
Paolo: knife (worn in a sheath at his waist)

Note: the banner should be fairly large, and on a pole. It should be divided into quarters. The quarters farthest from the pole, at the top, and nearest to it at the bottom, should be red, with the gold castle of Castile painted on them. The other two quarters should be white, painted with Aragon's red lion rampant.

LIGHTING PLOT

Property fittings required: nil
Various interior and exterior settings

To open: Overall general lighting

No cues